Women Moving Forward

How Ordinary Women Create Extraordinary Change

by

Pierrette Raymond

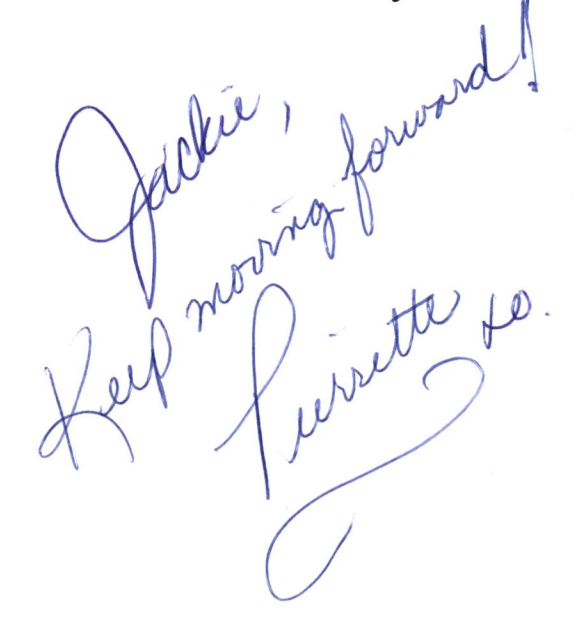

*Jackie,
Keep moving forward!
Pierrette xo.*

Book Coach Press

Women Moving Forward: How ordinary women create extraordinary change.
Copyright © 2003, Pierrette Raymond

Published by Book Coach Press
Canadian Office: Ottawa, Ontario
United States Office: Danville, California
www.BookCoachPress.com

All rights reserved. Reviewers and those referencing may quote brief passages from the book. Written permission to reproduce larger portions may be obtained from the author.

Pierrette Raymond
Telephone: (613) 841-3405
Email: info@womenmovingforward.ca
Website: www.womenmovingforward.ca

National Library of Canada Cataloguing in Publication

Raymond, Pierrette, 1969-
  Women moving forward: how ordinary women create extraordinary change / Pierrette Raymond.

ISBN 0-9680347-8-0

  1. Women--Psychology. 2. Self-management (Psychology)
3. Life change events. 4. Women Moving Forward. I. Title.

HQ1460.O88R39 2003   158.1'082   C2003-904830-6

Cover and Graphic Design: Evelyn Budd of Budd Graphics
Editing: Serena Williamson Andrew; Leslie Rubec
Cover photo: Jessie Parker

Printed in Canada

Contents

ACKNOWLEDGEMENTS		V
INTRODUCTION		IX
1.	THE FIRST MEETING	1
2.	WOMEN MOVING FORWARD—WHAT IS IT?	5
3.	PRINCIPLE # 1: RECONNECTING WITH YOURSELF	13
4.	PRINCIPLE # 2: GO FOR THE "GOALS"	29
5.	PRINCIPLE # 3: IT WON'T GET DONE UNLESS YOU DO IT!	39
6.	PRINCIPLE # 4: WHY DO IT ALONE?	43
7.	PRINCIPLE # 5: THE PROMISE OF CHANGE	51
8.	WHAT ARE YOU WAITING FOR?	57
9.	THE 90-DAY EMPOWERMENT ACTION PLAN WORKBOOK	63
EPILOGUE		83
ABOUT THE AUTHOR		85
PARTICIPANT BIOGRAPHIES		87

Acknowledgements

WHEN WOMEN MOVING FORWARD was founded in October 2002, the idea of a book was far beyond what I envisioned. It wasn't until I began learning more about myself and listening to my heart that I realized that the stories of the women needed to be shared.

Witnessing such incredible change in such a short time inspired me to share their stories to help inspire other women to fulfill their dreams.

Writing this book has been an incredible learning experience for me and my family. Together we learned patience, understanding and the real meaning of support.

My heartfelt thanks go first to my family. Luc, Joshua and Briana, you never tired when I told you I was working. You stayed patient and understanding of my purpose to create the book and you have been the light that has always guided me and kept me focused on the outcome. I am blessed to have you in my life. I thank God every day that you are "mine." Because of your undying love for me and your belief in me, I can follow my dreams and pursue my passion with you by my side. Thank you so very much! I love you!

To my father Ron Saudino, my mother Lucille Beauchamp-Saudino, to my mother and father-in-law Georgette and Bob Raymond, you never questioned my desire to do more, learn more and be more. Your support, encouragement and your belief in me have helped keep me focused on what was truly important for me and my family. I am so thankful and feel so blessed to have parents like you. Thank you!

Acknowledgements

To my sister-in-law Suzanne Leblanc, your love for life and your family have been inspiring to me. Although you are facing the most challenging time in your life, I believe in you and your strength. You inspire me and you motivate me and by sharing your story with other women, I'm sure you will inspire others to want and do more in their lives. Your light will forever shine in our hearts.

To a very dear friend of mine, Nicole Casey, who has always been an inspiration to me. your belief in me and what I envisioned was so very touching when we first sat down to give life to Women Moving Forward. You were the first person who helped me bring Women Moving Forward to life and I am eternally thankful for you Nicole. I am blessed to have you in my life.

To my personal coach Jackie Lauer who was always there to see more in me than I saw in myself. Your guidance, support, and undying passion to help motivate and inspire, kept me learning more about myself as I pulled from within the strength I needed to move forward. Because of you, I have been able to tame my "Gremlins" or turn to you when they appear! You are a wonderful coach, mentor and friend. Thanks Jac!

To our very first advisory group, Judith Cane, Janet Gray, Jackie Lauer, Melanie Arscott and Angela Sutcliff who can envision along with me all that Women Moving Forward can and will be. Without your help, guidance and support, I would be struggling to make my vision come to life. Thanks for being honest, sincere and interested in the success of Women Moving Forward.

To Serena Williamson Andrew, the best book coach there is! When we first met several months ago, I absolutely knew we

Acknowledgements

had met for a reason and that we were meant to work together on a project. This being my first had its challenges, but Serena, you never faltered. You continually supported, encouraged and believed in me. Without you Serena, this project would not have come to fruition. I am so thankful you are a part of my life, not only because we worked together on the creation of this book but because you touch people's hearts. You are a beautiful person whose light shines on everyone who meets you!

And finally, to the women of Women Moving Forward. I get emotional when I think of all I have learned from all of you. At each meeting, I stand before you and tell you that without you, I would be standing in a room by myself.

Because of what I learned from all of you, I have come to learn so much about myself. You fuel me to continue giving and helping women to move forward. I am living my life with passion and purpose and it is because of what I have learned from you! Cheers to you!

Introduction

WHAT IF SOMEONE TOLD YOU there was a key that would open doors to extraordinary change for you? What if you were told that key was in your hand right now?

This book tells the true stories of ordinary women who have taken ordinary steps to create extraordinary change in a short time. Each woman needed something and found it, almost by chance, during a process that allowed her to rediscover herself.

These ordinary women all have the same obligations and responsibilities we all share, and are continually striving for balance in their lives.

It is obvious from everything that you read and see, women today face many challenges that they didn't face before. They find themselves with too many responsibilities and very little time. They hurry through their daily routines ensuring they meet their many, varied obligations, often without realizing that they have the power to slow the pace, make conscious time for themselves, and live a more enriched and fulfilled life if they choose to be true to themselves.

The women you are about to meet are ordinary women. They have jobs and careers, own businesses and are entrepreneurs. What separates them is what they have accomplished in so little time. They are inspiring. They are motivating. They desire more for themselves and have just begun living that desire. They are creating their own calmness in their lives by focusing on what is truly important to them.

What you are about to read will start you on a journey of self-discovery. It is quite possible that you will find yourself in one

Introduction

of the stories. This book is meant to be a mirror for you and your own life; one that allows you to look deeply and see whether you are as pleased as you could be with your reflection.

This is also a book to inspire you. By reading the many engaging and thought-provoking stories, you will find yourself cheering for the women while moving forward yourself.

You will also be introduced to Women Moving Forward, the organization that began the wonderful process of change for these women. When Women Moving Forward was founded in October 2002, its mission was to help professional business and career women find balance in their lives by focusing not only on their careers but on their personal lives as well.

Women Moving Forward is a young organization, but its success is astonishing. It has benefited countless women through its newsletter, its monthly meetings and its "Girls' Night Outs." It is called Women Moving Forward because that is *exactly* what the women of the group are doing.

To move forward in life, we must take steps to move from one place to another, just as we do when walking. Women Moving Forward focuses on helping women move from one place to another in their lives, not on a physical scale, but more on an emotional and personal scale.

In looking at how a child learns to walk, we can see common elements with how we, as adults, move forward in our lives. When a child first tries to walk, standing itself is a challenge. Once that is mastered, the child then takes steps while holding onto things, followed by taking steps between two objects that are relatively close to one another. When ready, the child faces the direction he or she wants to go, takes initiative to move in that direction, and slowly and sometimes cautiously, takes the first step.

Introduction

Although a child is rarely able to walk very far the first time, his or her first steps bring immeasurable joy to the parents. With much encouragement and support, the child sees the parents' excitement and takes another step, followed by another, and then another. Before long, the child is walking.

Like encouraging the child to walk, Women Moving Forward has helped women take their first steps toward major, life-changing goals. Through the support of fellow members, women have accomplished things they never thought possible.

But how does this process work? How is Women Moving Forward different? How can it help you move forward in your own life? You have the answers in your hands right now. Women will tell you, in their own words, how they did it, how they moved forward, and how they created extraordinary change. These are the true stories of women who have shared their experiences to help you find your own way and move forward in your life.

Are you ready to begin the journey? Are you ready to discover how you too can create extraordinary change in your own life? Let's begin.

The first meeting

THE ROOM IS ALL RIGHT. It can seat 12 people but all I am hoping for is that five will show up. It is warm. If we were to fill the room, it would be much too hot in here. Perhaps I can open a door. Ah, but that won't work. It leads to the front desk of the recreation centre, and there is far too much traffic and noise out there.

The tables are in place. The sign-in area is ready. The coffee is brewing. Have I forgotten anything?

What am I doing? This question suddenly comes into my mind and I'm forced to listen to it. "What the heck are you doing?" I ask myself. "You're standing alone in this room and you're hoping that five people will come. Why do you think that even *one* person will? No one cares that you want to help women? No one cares what you're doing here tonight? No one will want to know what Women Moving Forward is, no one."

"Oh stop," I say to myself. "You have to try it. You have to give it a shot. It's something that is in you, and you know it. You know you have to at least give yourself the opportunity to see if it can work. Stop thinking of all the negatives and focus on what great things could happen."

As I stood there in front of an empty room, I imagined it filled with women, women who were laughing, talking and sharing stories with one another, and having a great time.

These women were businesswomen. They were professional women with careers. They were women who were enjoying taking a break from their busy lives to be at the meeting, to be together, to share and grow personally and professionally.

What a beautiful picture that was. My heart soared just at the thought. The picture was so clear. It was almost as though the women were really there, as though I was living the truth of what was, as though it were truly real.

Then the door opened. She was the first woman to walk in, a woman coming to see what Women Moving Forward was about. I was so happy. Someone actually came! As I greeted her, all my worries and anxieties melted away. The moment was happening, and the future started.

This is what it was like for me at the very first Women Moving Forward meeting. I was questioning myself as to why I had taken the steps to start a women's group. Who did I think I was? Why did I think that others could benefit from a group like this one? Could it really help other women? Could it be successful?

It has been seven months since that first meeting and so much has happened. So many wonderful and amazing women have created change in such a short amount of time. It is important to share it with you.

Women Moving Forward started as a thought several months ago, after two and a half years in a business that had started to drain me. It was a business that both my husband and I were involved in full-time. Even though we thoroughly enjoyed working side-by-side, my passion for the business had started to fade. The work had become very administrative and the personal rewards were no longer there.

Because I found working in the business no longer satisfying, things began to shift inside of me. I became untrue to myself, thinking things would improve if I only dedicated more time and effort to the "job." Then, I told myself, the passion would come back.

The first meeting

I had convinced myself that this business was the best thing for us and all I really needed to do was tuck away my feelings and force the passion back.

But what I didn't realize was that I was losing myself. I was living for everyone else except me, doing things for all of *them* and letting go of what *I* needed and wanted.

At least this way, I could still feel that I was giving to others. But this didn't work for long. I started feeling resentful and unhappy because I was letting go of what was important for *me*.

I don't know exactly when or how it happened, but I finally woke up. I began to pay attention to myself and to what my heart and soul were saying. They were telling me to get real and what I was doing with my life was not living my true passion. I knew I was unhappy inside and I had to do something about it, but what?

I felt trapped in a business that didn't fulfill me. The business was our only source of income and I just couldn't stop working. My husband and family depended on me to fulfill my obligations and continue to work in the business. I just had to stay involved. But how could I do that and still be who I needed to be? How could I work at something that was draining me and still do something that could help me be me?

Women Moving Forward was born a short time later. A combination of ideas and experiences brought Women Moving Forward to life.

My passion has always been to teach and help others. Since I was a little girl, I grew up knowing I would teach. Throughout my life I have been teaching in schools, offices and homes. My life's work has been teaching. It is part of me, it is in me and it will always be.

My desire to help others is a powerful strength. I am most happy when I am giving and making a difference in someone else's life. It fuels me and gives me energy. It drives me to do more.

Couple these two qualities with my leadership abilities and you have what has driven me to create Women Moving Forward. Women Moving Forward is an organization that is dedicated to helping women by educating and inspiring through its newsletter, its members, its speakers and its outings. It is an organization that is dedicated to lead women to define their own success and happiness and move forward to achieve it.

But there is more, there is much more. The women of Women Moving Forward have also taken steps to live their best lives. They are discovering for themselves how to align who they are, what they are doing with their lives, and where they are going. They have discovered their passions and have chosen to live their lives with more purpose.

As we take the journey of discovery with them, we will see what they have done to be so successful at realigning themselves with who they truly are. We will identify the principles that allowed them to create the change that enabled them to start doing what they felt most passionate about. And we will be inspired by their stories of accomplishment and self-discovery.

Through the principles and the stories, you will have the tools necessary to realign yourself with who you are, what you are doing and where you are going. You will able to put it all together and start living a more passionate and purposeful life.

Women Moving Forward
What is it?

"I'M TOO TIRED," MOANS LISA. "I don't feel like going out tonight. There's laundry to do. The dishwasher needs emptying. Timothy asked me to work on his project. Ahhh, if only I could just allow myself to go, to say it's ok to just go out and see what they are all about! Jackie said they were a fun group and that I would enjoy myself but I just have so much to do and I'm just so tired right now."

In the other room Lisa hears Timothy and Samantha arguing. They've been at it since she got home. The arguing and bickering is starting to get to her and she feels herself starting to boil. With the stress of work and what she has to do around the house, she's afraid she's going to lose it.

"Maybe I should just go. Maybe it will do me some good to get out for a night. I've had a long day at work and it would be nice to spend some time with Jackie." Lisa decides that she is going to go and tells her family she's going out to a meeting, a Women Moving Forward meeting.

"Women Moving Forward," she mumbles to herself. "How interesting. I know I'm moving forward all the time. At least I think I am. Jackie said it was a fun night out and since going to her first meeting, she has noticed things changing for her. I just have to go check this out for myself."

As she approaches the door to the room where the meeting is being held, Lisa feels a little nervous. She knows there will be other women there, women she doesn't know. She knows this is going to be all new to her. As she opens the door and walks in she is surprised to see so *many women talking, laughing and moving about. Women are smiling and laughing and they all seem to be enjoying themselves.*

"Hi! My name is Janet. I believe this could be your first time here. Come on in."

Immediately Lisa calms as she is greeted by such a warm and inviting woman.

This is the scenario of many women who come to Women Moving Forward for the first time. They struggle to give themselves permission to attend and have to juggle family commitments before being able to leave their homes. Once the structure is in place however, the stage is set. The women enter the Women Moving Forward meeting and feel the air buzzing with excitement. They know that they are in for a night that will nourish them both personally and professionally. They know that what they can expect is a night out, to be free of their everyday stresses and responsibilities and enjoy their "me" time.

How is Women Moving Forward so different from all other meetings? How has it become such a meaningful part of so many women's lives? The answer lies in the openness and enthusiasm of the women who attend, and a creative structure that allows the best in these women to come out and be nourished.

A TASTE OF WOMEN MOVING FORWARD

Under the expert guidance of a caring, trained facilitator, every woman has an opportunity to introduce herself to the other women in the group. This is her time to share who she is and get to know the other women in the room. From this very moment, the women begin to build relationships with one another. They learn about things they have in common and develop a rapport.

"Hi. My name is Lisa. I am a loan officer at ABC Bank and have been working in the banking industry for 15 years. I am married and have two adolescent children, who were almost driving me to a boiling point this evening. Their bickering was just starting to get to me and I knew I had to get out. So I came here, to you."

The women chuckle and smile understanding what it is like. They congratulate her for coming out.

The woman sitting next to Lisa introduces herself and says she has grown children and knows exactly what Lisa is going through. She remembers and tells Lisa that it too will pass and they will grow up and move out. And then the women applaud jokingly.

Throughout the introductions, Lisa is moved by the stories of the other women in the room. She is surprised by the wide age range and diverse careers. From a professional standpoint, she is enthralled by the potential for new clients. From a personal standpoint, she looks forward to learning more about the fascinating women she has just met.

Following the introductions, the facilitator explains that the next part of the meeting is all about Goal Sharing. She points to the Goal Cards laid out on the table and explains the three categories found on each card.

Lisa picks up a card and listens attentively. This is the first time she has ever been given a Goal Card. She looks down and sees categories, each followed by lots of blank space. The Goal Card objectives come clear to her as the facilitator continues. Lisa learns that at every meeting each woman ponders her life and selects three goals for herself, goals she will try to reach before the next meeting two weeks hence. The first line reads *Health and Fitness*, the second, *Business and Career*, and the third, *Humanitarian*.

The meeting facilitator then invites the women to share their goals from the previous meeting and talk about their "hits and misses."

One woman immediately volunteers. "I set a *Health and Fitness* goal to walk three times since our last meeting and I walked four times!" The group erupts with applause. "I also set a *Business and Career* goal to contact six previous clients, but I only contacted three." The women applaud again. One woman shouts, "Hey, that's 50 percent of your goal!" The women laugh and cheer. "And my last goal, my *Humanitarian* goal, was to send an old friend a card saying I was thinking of her, and I did that too." The women applaud again, sincerely celebrating her accomplishments.

Woman after woman share their goals and their "hits and misses" and each time, the women applaud and recognize the woman's efforts. In every instance the woman's face lights up with gratitude.

Lisa is in awe. She is amazed how much the women support one another. Jackie did mention that goals were set and shared, but Lisa didn't expect this. She didn't expect to "feel" this. This is what the buzz was about at the beginning of the meeting. This is what she sensed as she entered the room. These women were being acknowledged, supported and praised for who they were and what they were doing. Lisa felt wonderfully warm inside. She had already started thinking of some goals she could set and share with the group at her next meeting.

Setting goals is not something that is new to most people. Most of us have set goals before. But what is different with the goals the women set at Women Moving Forward meetings is that they are very focused and have clear and measurable outcomes. They are goals that have been chosen because each woman is working toward living her life with more passion and purpose. The goals are designed to bring her the success that she desires.

We have discussed the introductions and goal setting cards, and, apart from the tea and cookies, there is one more aspect of each meeting that makes Women Moving Forward what it is. The women have an opportunity at each meeting to be moved, inspired and educated by two guest speakers who each have the floor for 20 minutes. The guest speakers and their topics are chosen specifically to nurture the women and evoke the desire in each of them to live their lives more fully.

Combining both the sharing of goals and the powerful messages being delivered by the speakers, the participants of Women Moving Forward become empowered by the experience of each meeting. Their souls are nourished as they begin to take notice of themselves, their needs and their desires.

By listening to their hearts, their inner selves, they begin to set goals that focus on their passions and they begin to develop their purpose. Their inner voice emerges more at each meeting, coming forth and guiding the women to set goals that have powerful and clear outcomes.

As soon as the second speaker finished, Lisa wrote on her Goal Card. She was moved. She had heard her inner voice speak and started thinking of things she had wanted to do for a long time but "never got around to it." She began to envision the future and saw that there was more in life for her than she had thought. In listening to the speakers, and the other women, she found herself wanting more. She knew she could do it.

She looked at the Goal Card and set her *Health and Fitness* goal. She wrote down that she would dust off the treadmill and use it twice this week. That was realistic. With her scheduled workweek, she didn't want to commit to something she knew she couldn't do. She could walk on the treadmill twice for 20 minutes. She also wrote that she would drink more water every day and add one fruit to her lunch every other day. Those goals were realistic. She could accomplish them.

She then focused on her *Business and Career* goal. She knew her office was not as tidy as she would like it to be. She thought that would be a good goal to start with. She would commit to doing all the filing the day she received it. She knew on some days she would finish late and might run into a problem completing her goal but she wanted to give it a try. If she could keep up with her filing and keep her office organized, she would be happy with her goal.

She struggled with her *Humanitarian* goal. She was unsure if she wanted to donate any money to a charity, and she didn't have the time this week for volunteering. The meeting facilitator had said that being humanitarian meant being more caring, thoughtful and compassionate to other human beings. She heard that one woman helped an elderly man carry his groceries to his car. This was so new to her that she wanted her first *Humanitarian* goal to simply be more aware of the kind and caring things she could do for others that she otherwise would have overlooked. She wrote down, "I commit to being more aware in order to be more humanitarian." Lisa was happy with her first three goals and was anxious to share them with the group.

As she listened to the other women share their goals, she thought how wonderful it was to be part of such a dynamic and powerful group of women. Hearing about the others' goals was inspiring to Lisa. She knew she would not be alone as she worked toward her goals. All the other women were doing the same thing. She felt empowered and excited about all that was being accomplished by her new group of friends and colleagues.

When it was her turn to share, Lisa confidently read her goals and immediately felt supported. All nodded, sincerely acknowledging her goals, and Lisa felt great. She was ready to go.

As the meeting came to a close, Lisa was so happy that she attended. She thought of the things she would have done instead and was immediately thrilled she took part in her first Women Moving Forward meeting. There was nothing like it, and she knew she would return.

On her way home, Lisa couldn't stop thinking of all the things she wanted to do. One of the speakers had touched her heart and made her begin to realize that she could want and do more with her life. Lisa wanted to listen to her heart and soul. She wanted to be more in touch with who she really was. She wanted to start taking action on the things that nourished her. She simply felt more alive.

When she walked in the door, her husband immediately noticed the smile on her face. "Good meeting?" he asked. "Fantastic!" Lisa confessed. "I'll definitely be going back. The next meeting is in two weeks and I'm looking forward to it."

Lisa told her husband about her evening, how she had met some incredible women, how she listened to women who had set goals at their last meeting and then shared their accomplishments. She explained how the group was so supportive and encouraging. She told him that she laughed and had a wonderful time. She also spoke about the speakers and how one of them truly moved her. She showed him her Goal Card and shared her goals. Her husband was impressed.

Lisa placed the Goal Card on the refrigerator and smiled. She knew what a wonderful journey she was beginning.

Principle # 1
Reconnecting with yourself

IN THE PREVIOUS CHAPTER, YOU MET LISA. She is a fictional character but her story reflects how most women describe their first experiences with Women Moving Forward. They become energized and realize that there is so much more they desire and can achieve.

Now you will meet Carmen. Her first experience was cautious and guided. She had just completed a long work project and was at a transitional time in her life. However, it didn't take Carmen long to realize the impact her first experience would have on her.

Carmen

Before Women Moving Forward, I was in transition. I had just completed a very long and arduous project that took a lot out of me, and I needed some time to find myself again, to discover what my options were and what opportunities there were for me in the community.

I saw an ad in the newspaper for Women Moving Forward and the name caught my attention. I instinctively knew that I would benefit from connecting with other women. I knew that I wanted to learn more about life and perhaps experience Women Moving Forward.

My first meeting held mixed feelings for me. Initially, I honestly did not want to attend. I worried that it would become another long project; one I didn't have the time, energy or desire to do.

However, during the first meeting, I felt good. I felt welcomed and relaxed and I enjoyed my time surrounded by other positive women. I was still trying to determine if this would be a good fit for me because many women had businesses and I thought this was a networking meeting, but I knew I wanted to come back. The energy in the room was far too great to not experience again.

As I attended a few more meetings, I saw that I was benefiting from being part of the group. I had become quite inspired and I started to become more confident. Just hearing about the other women, their goals, and their accomplishments has encouraged and given me more confidence. "If they can do it, so can I," I thought.

I have grown so much and have done so many new things since I became part of the group, things I would not have accomplished had it not been for the influence of Women Moving Forward and my newfound belief in myself.

I began to set new goals for myself. I began mentoring immigrants to Canada through an online mentoring program. Through this initiative, I am able to offer my skills to others and help them transition into our country. I have also become involved in two organizations in which I volunteer two hours per month. This has nourished me and given me so much strength.

I am most proud of the women's peer-mentoring program I have developed and am now coordinating. I look forward to continually growing personally and professionally. I would not have tried new things had it not been for Women Moving Forward.

I have certainly moved forward in my life. I have experienced both personal and professional development and I have enjoyed watching other women go through similar changes. I have found it extremely positive in my life, and I truly feel it keeps me aligned and committed every single day!

Principle # 1: Reconnecting with yourself

When Carmen came to her first Women Moving Forward meeting, she felt physically and emotionally drained. Her spirit was tired and she needed time to rethink her personal goals, and redefine who she was and what she wanted. Carmen needed to find her self again.

At her first meeting, Carmen began to reconnect with her self. The friendliness of the group, the relaxed feeling it provided, and the positive outlook the women had were very encouraging for Carmen, something she needed after a long journey in her life. Carmen knew she could find what she needed in this group.

Carmen felt inspired by the women. She listened to them share their own experiences and challenges. She was able to see herself in some of their experiences and draw strength from knowing she wasn't alone.

She also became more confident and was able to motivate and inspire other women in the group. What she wasn't aware of was that she too was giving strength, support and encouragement to other women just by being who she was.

Many women feel disconnected, alone and in need of rediscovering who they are. Our work often requires us to do things that are not aligned with what we love and value. Forced to make choices that impinge on our own sense of being, we feel frustrated and dispirited.

Carmen found support in Women Moving Forward during a transitional time. She needed to reconnect with herself and with others. The friendliness and warmth she experienced was the catalyst for her. It began a new process of focus for Carmen, one that included listening to her inner voice for the answers she needed to hear.

Carmen was moved to action, taking steps to move forward and do the things her heart was telling her she could do. She listened, took action and got results. Week after week, she continued to set goals that were important to her. She focused on being empowered by the results her goals would bring. As she did this, she could see more in herself than she did before.

Carmen's decision to find her self again allowed her to move forward. She has begun to live her life with more passion and purpose and is inspiring others to do the same. Women applaud her accomplishments and encourage her to pursue her endeavors. Carmen has truly created extraordinary and empowering change in her own life.

GETTING TO KNOW YOU: THE FIVE-STEP WOMEN MOVING FORWARD PROCESS

Step One: Listen to your heart and soul

The women of Women Moving Forward create extraordinary and empowering success because they become clear about who they are as they begin to listen to their inner selves. They become clear about what they are doing in their daily lives as they measure it against their true passion. In doing so, they live their lives with more purpose.

It is a process that we have seen happen repeatedly. The structure of the meetings, the women of the groups and the speakers give the women an opportunity to listen and pay attention to who they really are.

Have you ever noticed that many people go through life and really never "get it"? There seems to be an ever-growing number of people wandering from one thing to another, from one place to another, without having meaning to their journey.

Principle # 1: Reconnecting with yourself

Women Moving Forward helps women to stop wandering aimlessly. It provides an opportunity to stop, listen to what the soul is saying, and move forward toward living life more purposefully and passionately. You too can achieve this.

It can be frightening to not know who you are, like Carmen who needed to rediscover her self. Perhaps you are looking for that as well. Perhaps you are looking for something that will bring more meaning to your life.

The truth is you already have it. You already have it in you, that "something" that will refocus you. You simply need to listen to your heart to realize how truly different and unique you are. You are unlike anyone else with your own wonderful characteristics, traits, strengths and weaknesses. You are gifted with your uniqueness and your individuality.

Take the following test. Close your eyes and put your hand on your heart. Pull every thought and every feeling into that hand. Now, feel the power of what is inside you, at this very moment. Feel it. Listen to it. Pay attention.

Be sure to get out of your head. Don't listen to what your head is saying about what you are doing. Listen with your heart. Ground yourself with your hand on your heart and truly feel your own inner power.

There is something powerful that occurs when people place their hand on their heart. The power of their own being grounds them. It centres them. It brings them to their core.

And you are truly "being" when you are at your core; when you are truly experiencing your inner self. It's almost magical. It certainly is powerful. That is where the power of the human spirit lives; inside your self, inside your own heart.

The women of Women Moving Forward have an opportunity at every meeting to connect with their inner self. When they hear of other women realizing their dreams and accomplishing their goals, they become in tune with what is important to them.

When a speaker encourages the women to question themselves and pay attention to their soul, they connect with the core of their being. And it's not until the women do that, truly listen to their hearts, that they find the answers to the questions of who they are, what they are doing and where they are going. They must be able to tap into themselves to find these answers. And you can too.

In order to tap into the human spirit, doing the exercise mentioned above—grounding yourself with your hand on your heart—is a beginning.

Listening to what your soul is saying comes next. This takes a little discipline. It's easy to ignore or overlook what the soul is saying because of all the outside noises and influences that bombard us daily. There is too much noise, too much else to pay attention to, too many outside influences drowning out our inner voice. It's easy to not hear it, even when it is screaming at us to pay attention.

It often occurs when a person has "intuition" or a "gut feeling" about something. They wonder what is causing it and then blow it off without paying attention. They continue without listening when all along it was their inner voice, their own self talking to them, pleading with them to listen.

To overcome the outside noises and listen to your soul, you must truly pay attention, and take the time to listen. When you are quiet with your self, you can ask questions that will bring forth answers to guide you to live your life with more

Principle # 1: Reconnecting with yourself

passion and purpose. The questions will force you to deeply mine what is inside you.

Some questions are easier to answer than others. Answers may come up almost instantaneously because they are things that you already know and trust. Other questions may require more internal research. The answers are buried deep within and have not yet been discovered, or have been put away for a long time. Doing the internal research takes time, dedication and desire.

Step Two: Who Am I?

There are countless books and articles that help people define who they are. What is being offered here is an opportunity to participate in what the women of Women Moving Forward have been experiencing since its inception; to see, hear and feel what they discovered.

The following exercise will provide an opportunity for you to tune into your inner self, and pay attention to what it is saying. Your answers will reveal some things that you already know and perhaps shed light on areas you hadn't thought of. The exercise can take a few minutes or hours – it's up to you. It is the start to experiencing the extraordinary changes of Women Moving Forward.

You can do this exercise and the ones to follow mentally, however writing down your answers in the workbook at the back of this book can help you develop a powerful roadmap to your future.

Read the following questions one at a time. Close your eyes, place your hand on your heart and take a deep breath as you ask yourself each question. Pay attention to the images you see, the sounds you hear and the feelings that surface. Pay close attention to what your soul is showing and telling. Take a few moments to let it all surface and if you begin to shift focus or start thinking of another thought, come back, repeat the question and if nothing new surfaces, stop. Now, write down everything you saw, heard and felt. Make it as detailed as possible using descriptive words that will capture what you experienced. Once you have completed one question, move on to the next.

For example, here are some answers that may surface:

Personality traits:
Happy, joyous, giving, nurturing, thoughtful

Qualities:
Sociable, committed, compassionate, caring

Enjoy doing:
Being with other people, helping, sharing, having fun, being with family, reading

A few words of caution: do not judge what surfaces. Do not try to correct what is coming out. Do not criticize or remove anything that you saw, heard or felt. Keep it all and write it all down. It may all be important once the process has been completed.

Let's begin.

What are your personality traits?

What are your qualities?

What do you enjoy doing?

What fulfills you?

What excites you?

What are you passionate about?

Principle # 1: Reconnecting with yourself

What do you desire?

What are your strengths?

What empowers you?

What motivates you?

When do you feel you are at your best? What are you doing?

When are you most happy? What are you doing?

What makes you different from everyone else?

What does your legacy look like? What do you want people to say and remember about you when you are gone or passed?

What do you want to be remembered for?

Once you have answered the questions, the next step is to find the common elements in the answers. A clearer picture will begin to emerge. You become the artist and this is your painting, a painting of your soul.

In the example below, we have underlined the common elements.

Personality traits:
Happy, joyous, giving, nurturing, thoughtful

Qualities:
Sociable, committed, compassionate, caring

Enjoy doing:
Being with other people, helping, sharing, having fun, being with family, reading

What begins to stand out and take shape is a clear picture of who you are.

As you look at the example, you can see from just the first three questions that this person enjoys being with others in a role that helps and contributes.

At this stage, some people experience an "aha" moment, as a rush of emotion overpowers them. They begin to internalize what they have just experienced because the words they have written painted a unique and masterful picture. For some, this confirms what they already knew. It brings comfort and peace and provides encouragement. For others, it begins a journey of self-discovery. It provides an opportunity to discover, learn, and appreciate who they are. It brings new focus and light to their lives. It begins a journey of newfound happiness and fulfillment.

Others may be scared and intimidated, filled with concern and doubt. This process may have uncovered something they did not know, something frightening. They may fear having to redefine who they are and realign what they thought they knew. If this is you, as it was with many members of Women Moving Forward, take a few deep breaths and stay with us. Some of our members' most fabulous results came from stepping into the fearful unknown.

Step Three: Finding meaning

Once you have identified and recognized the common elements in your answers to the questions, you must give meaning to what you discovered. This requires owning and accepting what you have found. Grab hold of it! Feel it! Embrace it! It has come from within, from your inner self, and it belongs. Allow yourself to be enveloped by all its meaning.

Once you take ownership of what has surfaced, a powerful thing happens. You begin to shift, to believe; believe in the words on the paper and ultimately, believe in yourself. Logically, that is what should happen. The words on the paper simply reflect your internal voice. It's your own truth. Knowing who you are is powerful. With that power, you can determine if what you are doing aligns with who you are. It may not require drastic changes to align the two; it may simply involve recognizing some differences and allowing small changes to occur.

For some, being in alignment may require more than a few simple changes. It may require a complete re-evaluation of their life. It's not an easy thing to do. Difficult choices may have to be made. Difficult observations may come into play. Facing reality can be hard and require a desire to understand and appreciate what choices are available and what the end results could be. Having faith and confidence is what gets most people through this step.

Refusing to accept what the true inner self is saying leads to living an incongruent life. Balance is almost impossible and true happiness is unachievable. The inconsistencies of living and doing without being true to one's self can be frustrating, disappointing, discouraging, and cause pain, misery and ill health.

Listen to what your heart and soul are saying. Accept and embrace it. Once you begin to take ownership you will feel a shift and begin to experience the powerful changes the women of Women Moving Forward experience.

Step Four: What am I doing?
Aligning who you are with what you are doing

Listening to your inner voice and aligning it with what you are doing will empower you. It will allow you to live a life filled with pleasures and accomplishments because you are being true to who you really are.

Once you begin to live your life in synch with who you are, like the women in Women Moving Forward, you too will enjoy the glorious feeling of your unyielding spirit. You will experience new breath as you realize the power of being who you are and not what you think you're supposed to be.

To begin aligning your self with what you are doing now, you must first realize and celebrate that you are doing things that are already aligned with who you truly are. You are already doing things that you are passionate about, that excite and empower you. Recognize this and celebrate it, as did the women of Women Moving Forward. Not one woman comes to a meeting expecting to change her entire life. What the women discover is that there are more nourishing things that they can do to feel more complete, more excited, more empowered and more in tune.

As they found themselves discovering the possibilities and their own true potential, the women became more passionate about their own lives and began to move forward to empowering change.

What are the things you are now doing that you are passionate about? What are the things that you are doing that fuel you and excite you? Write them down and celebrate them.

What are some of the things that you are doing in your life that do not fulfill you, that are not aligned with your true self? Write them down as well and notice how you feel about them.

It is not wrong to be living a life that is not completely congruent. Most people are living that way. There's imbalance and frustration. There are feelings of inadequacy and stress, perhaps not in all areas but in some. It is important to realize that these areas can become aligned again. It takes realizing that they are not and it takes a desire to change.

The natural question to follow is how can that be done? How can you realign who you are with what you do? The answer: decide to do it!

Principle # 1: Reconnecting with yourself

When people want to realign who they are with what they are doing to become more satisfied, more fulfilled, more empowered, the decision has to be made that they are going to do it. They want to live a congruent life. They want to experience all the rewards that such a life brings. Without desire, it simply is a want. It will not materialize or happen. There must be determination and a true desire for the end result.

When you look at your personal inventory from the earlier exercise, you can clearly see if what you are doing is aligned with who you are. For example, if you are passionate about helping and interacting with people and you are working alone in a cubicle all day with no interaction with others, you will feel empty and unsatisfied. If this were you, you would need to look for opportunities to work in an environment that had direct interaction with people and involved helping and serving them. Surely you would then find yourself much happier.

Align your self with what you are doing and identify where and how you are already living in accordance with your true self. Know that most people live part of their lives in alignment with their inner spirit. They enjoy the benefits of living a life that reflects to a certain degree who they are. But most find pockets of emptiness and lack of fulfillment. In identifying those pockets, you too can fill the gaps by looking for opportunities to enrich your life.

When the women of Women Moving Forward listened to their inner selves, they saw the things they could do to move them toward living more empowering and purposeful lives.

You have the ability to see if you are currently living true to your self and identify opportunities that will enrich your life.

Step Five: Putting it all together
Determining life's purpose

When you begin to take action and align who you are with what you are doing, you will begin to determine your life's purpose.

When a person does not have clear purpose in life, loneliness, sadness and emptiness are omnipresent. Life becomes routine, unrewarding, dull and fruitless.

When passion enters a person's life, a whole new picture emerges. The person is vibrant, energetic, excited and a joy to be around. This person exudes confidence and mastery. Life is purposeful and fun.

The women of Women Moving Forward have discovered this powerful phenomenon. As they listen to their inner self and pay attention to what their soul is saying, they discover opportunities that move them toward living their life more purposefully and with more passion. They become more excited, energetic and enthusiastic about life.

CREATING THE ROADMAP

At every meeting, the women of Women Moving Forward set goals that focus on powerful and measurable outcomes. They understand the importance of these goals in creating substantial life changes.

In the next chapter, we will summarize what the women have learned and give you the tools to create your own roadmap to a more empowering and purposeful life.

Principle # 1: Reconnecting with yourself

- *Choose to live your life by being fulfilled, enriched and excited by your passion and your purpose.*

- *To define your passion and purpose, listen to your heart. Feel the power of what is inside you. Listen to it. Embrace it.*

- *Identify your strengths and weaknesses and choose to live your life more aligned with who you are.*

- *Acknowledge and celebrate how you are already living part of your life in alignment with your true spirit, your true self.*

- *Acknowledge and accept changes you would like to make to live your life in alignment with who you are.*

- *Be passionate about your life! Choose to live your life aligned with who you are, what you are doing and where you are going so you can enjoy living your life with purpose.*

Principle #2
Go for the "Goals"

UNDERSTAND THAT WHERE YOU ARE TODAY IS EXACTLY WHERE YOU ARE SUPPOSED TO BE.

To move forward, you must first have a clear understanding of where you are today and accept it as it being exactly where you are supposed to be.

At the meetings, the women are praised for who they are and where they are in their lives. They are celebrated for their uniqueness and individuality. They clearly appreciate the present and what they have accomplished thus far. They understand and accept that their life is exactly where it needs to be.

In creating your roadmap, you are shifting your focus from the "doing" to the "being." You develop a course of action based on who you are, your passion and your purpose.

Week after week, the women of Women Moving Forward make progress on their personal roadmaps. They set goals and take action toward achieving them. Following this roadmap is how they stay true to themselves.

To develop a roadmap, you must first identify where it is you would like to go. What is the outcome you are looking to achieve? What accomplishments are you striving to fulfil? What will you do to live your life with more passion and purpose?

GOALS ARE THE KEY TO A SUCCESSFUL ROADMAP

"Goals" is a simple word, a common word, one that is seen and heard daily. But its power is remarkable. When the women began setting goals, they began to find direction. The goals gave meaning and focus. And when the goals aligned with who the women truly were, the outcomes were significant, almost magical.

The women witnessed it time and time again. They realized how setting clear and realistic goals created extraordinary results and that almost anything could be achieved. They understood the power of having clear, concise and reasonable goals. They saw it. They experienced it. They lived it.

RACHEL'S DEFINING PURPOSE

I have always considered myself "happy-go-lucky," and yet, I've always dealt with a lack of confidence in myself. I always would question myself and say "if only I...." I found myself holding back on many opportunities because of my self-restricting fears.

When I saw an ad for Women Moving Forward for the first time, I thought how wonderful the timing in my life was for this to be happening. I had been struggling to get out of a job that didn't fulfill me. I wanted to do more with my life and the job I had wasn't getting me there.

At my first meeting I felt quite nervous. I was worried what people would think of me, I worried that I wasn't the right kind of woman to be at the meeting. I was shy and didn't feel I would fit in the group.

But I was so surprised by how welcomed I felt the moment I walked into the room. There was a very warm feeling and it didn't take me long to feel more comfortable. As the meeting progressed, I became

Principle # 2: Go for the "Goals"

more and more inspired and started to feel my own dreams come alive inside of me.

The speaker was a woman who had opened her own personal fitness centre. And as I listened to her speak, my inner voice started to speak to me. I knew I wanted to do what she had chosen to do with her life.

I spent some time following the meeting talking to her and was immediately impressed by how much work it took for her to become successful. This was what I wanted to do with my life. I have always wanted to be a personal fitness instructor and have my own gym. I knew that if she could do it, I could do it too!

Since that first meeting, I have greatly changed. My entire life's focus has changed. I am now so energized and excited about what the future can bring, and this is all because of what I experienced through Women Moving Forward.

I have become more inspired, more pumped and more in touch with what I want to do. The experience has been so positive and so inspiring that it feeds my desire to do more for myself.

Seeing other women achieve their goals has inspired me to put my own goals into perspective and to act upon them. I no longer wait for the opportunity — I create it. I used to find myself resisting change and pulling back from opportunities. Now I crave them! I want to move forward! I want to live my life doing what I love most!

In the past three months, so much has changed. I am writing down my goals and tracking my own success. I have started to teach aerobics and this is something I always wanted to do but felt too shy to even try. I am doing it regularly and truly loving it!

The energy I am experiencing releases my fears and allows me to step out of my comfort zone and try new things. I have even taught a cardio class when this was something I thought would take me a long time to do. I have done it!

Every day I feel ready! I feel excited and passionate! I feel I'm living my dream.

Every day, I look at the little things and appreciate them more.

I have this burning desire inside of me. I want to explore more. I want to do more. I want to continually try to do new things.

It is obvious in reading Rachel's experience that she has become more alive and in touch with who she truly is. She has paid attention to her inner voice and started to take action to living her life by following her passion. She has become clear on her purpose.

Before Women Moving Forward, Rachel was shy and lacked the self-confidence to pursue her passion. She had always wanted to lead and teach aerobic classes and yet never took the steps to fulfill her dream. She also dreamt of owning her own fitness facility and yet, she never acted upon what was most important to her, her true desire, her true passion.

Being at the Women Moving Forward meetings and setting goals has awakened Rachel's passion for living. She seriously looked at her life and listened to her heart. Rachel's heart was screaming at her to step out of her comfort zone and move forward toward her goals. She took action to live the life she has always wanted to live.

Rachel experienced tremendous personal growth. She has taken classes, begun working with a professional trainer and she has even conducted her very own fitness classes, all from listening to her own heart and following through on her goals.

Rachel's youth, vitality and desire to listen to her self and create her own destiny are truly inspirational to other women. The power of goals setting is evident in Rachel's story. Knowing who you are and what you want to do enables you

Principle # 2: Go for the "Goals"

to set clear goals to lead you to where you want to go. It's a matter of listening to your inner spirit and aligning your goals with who you truly are.

Setting goals is not always an easy process. It requires thought, listening to your internal spirit and paying attention to what you truly want to achieve.

If a goal is based on someone else's want or need it is highly unlikely that the satisfaction in achieving the goal will be heartfelt, if at all. Striving to attain a goal that is not aligned with who you are will be difficult and will cause a derailment of your purpose. You will feel empty and drained following the completion of the goal, rather than satisfied, excited and fulfilled.

When the women of Women Moving Forward set their goals, they ensure that they are being true to themselves. They ground themselves and listen to what is important. That is when they achieve extraordinary and empowering change.

HOW S.A.F.E. IS YOUR PURPOSE?

When goals are set following passion and purpose, the results are powerful and purposeful.

When setting your goals, remember to set S.A.F.E. goals.

Self—they come from within, from your inner self, your heart and soul

Align with self, with who you are

Focus—clear objectives, feel the power of the outcome

Empower! Excite! Energize!

When you set a goal that comes from your *self*, from within your own inner spirit, and you clearly align it with who you are, what you are doing and where you are going, your goal will bring you empowering results.

When a goal is set without *alignment* with one's true self, challenges may occur, outside influences may sidetrack its focus, and the end result will be less than favourable. The best goals are set when a person is true to oneself and one's purpose. These are the goals that are achieved naturally. They are "in sync" with the person's purpose and all fall into place.

When setting a goal, ensure you have a strong and clear *focus*. Without focus, there is no target, no focal point. A goal needs to have a clear outcome, a quantifiable result. Know what the end result will be, envision it, and know its purpose. When you envision the outcome of your goal, you are drawn to the result. Envisioning the end result solidifies and gives life to your goal.

And finally, a goal needs to *empower, excite and energize*. If setting a goal does none of the above, the goal becomes a task that seems more like a burden. A goal that empowers, excites and energizes is far more likely to be achieved. It has its own life and fuels you to want to achieve it. Being empowered by a goal is nourishing to the spirit. It drives the focus and the desire, and it allows you to feel the entire experience. An empowering goal is one that will keep you going the distance. It drives you to continue through all the challenges and obstacles. It becomes the force that keeps the momentum going.

In Rachel's story, we clearly saw how her goals were S.A.F.E. They were goals that followed this principle and because of it, created extraordinary success.

Her goals were created from within, from her desire to want more and accomplish more, and from her true passion for

Principle # 2: Go for the "Goals"

fitness and what she could do for others while teaching and leading fitness classes.

Rachel's goals were aligned with who she was, what she was doing and where she was going. She always wanted to teach aerobics and educate herself in this industry. She wanted to own her own fitness facility. However, what she was doing initially did not align with who she was. She was working at an unsatisfactory job that did not contribute to the inner voice that was calling her to become involved in her passion. She was actually stressed and wanting to leave.

When she aligned her goals with what she was doing, she stepped out of her comfort zone and looked for opportunities to do what she wanted to do. She created opportunities by setting goals and looking for what was available for her to achieve them. She asked to instruct classes. She was invited by others to teach in their absence. She was able to accomplish her goal by aligning herself with what she wants to be doing, with what her inner self was pleading her to do.

Rachel's goals also had clear focus. She knew exactly what she wanted to do. She wrote the goals down, she gave them life, and she focused on achieving them. They were very clear objectives with outcomes she could almost taste. Her goals empowered, energized and excited her. She was living her life wanting to achieve more. She was excited every day and knew she could accomplish her goals because they were S.A.F.E.

Setting S.A.F.E. goals allowed Rachel to experience extraordinary success. She is staying true to her self; she is aligning her goals with who she is, what she is doing and where she wants to go. She has a clear focus in each goal, and they truly empower, energize and excite her.

CREATING YOUR OWN S.A.F.E. GOALS

As with the women of Women Moving Forward, you may find yourself wanting to re-evaluate your goals and align them more with what your inner self is saying. Again, you can do this exercise mentally, however writing down your goals will have more impact. You may have started using the workbook at the back of the book or you may begin to use it now. There will be an opportunity to create a "90-Day Action Plan" using your goals and the workbook.

To create your own S.A.F.E. goals, find a quiet space, ground yourself with your hand on your heart and listen to your inner voice.

After my first Women Moving Forward meeting, I went home and sat in the tub until 1 a.m. with a pack of "Post-It" notes, writing down all of my "big ideas," my big goals. They were flooding me as they came to the surface and I quickly wrote them all down. It was a powerful exercise and I became clear on what I need to do to accomplish and achieve them. I was able to achieve clarity with this exercise. Because of the distinct clarity I had, I have been able to make my "big ideas" and my goals come to life.

Pauline identified her goals when she spent the time alone listening to herself. Through the exercise, she gained distinct clarity and focus.

What is your soul telling you? What goals do you want to accomplish? What is your passion and what can you to do to live it every day? Listen to your soul, to your inner self and the goals that are yours, and yours alone, will surface.

Ensure the goals are aligned with who you are, what you are doing and where you are going. If the goal does not align with all three, what can you do now to align it with what is going

Principle # 2: Go for the "Goals"

on in your life? How can it become a part of who you are and what you are doing and have a positive impact on where you are going? This may take some thinking and brainstorming but it can be done – because it comes from within you. Believe in your self, your inner spirit. The outcome of the goal should have a positive impact on where you are going.

When you have the goal, determine its focus. What is the outcome of the goal? What will you achieve by accomplishing it? What satisfaction will you have when you achieve it? And most importantly, how does it directly improve where you are going? What is the positive impact on where you are headed in your life?

Ensure that the goals you set and the roadmap you create, empower you. Ensure your goals excite and energize you. If they do not, you may struggle along the way to accomplish them.

Like Pauline and Rachel, and the other women of Women Moving Forward, make your goals S.A.F.E. Ensure they come from listening to your self, that they align with who you truly are, that they focus on clear outcomes, and that they empower and excite you. It is these goals that will bring you the most empowering and extraordinary success.

Principle # 2: Go for the "Goals"

- *Accept that where you are today is exactly where you are supposed to be.*
- *Give clear focus to your daily actions by creating powerful, empowering goals.*
- *Listen to your 'self', your inner voice and set goals that will bring your dreams to life. Create your roadmap using your goals.*
- *Set S.A.F.E. goals*
  - *Self — they come from within, from your inner self, your heart and soul.*
  - *Align with self, with who you are*
  - *Focus — clear objectives, feel the power of the outcome*
  - *Empower! Excite! Energize!*
- *Visualize the outcome. See where you want to be, ensuring that your desired future is aligned with your purpose.*

Principle # 3
It won't get done unless you do it!

ALTHOUGH SETTING GOALS is a big step toward creating extraordinary change, many goals are set, yet never accomplished. What makes the difference? Action! Without action, nothing gets done.

People often set goals and feel energized and excited. Who hasn't made a long list of New Year's Resolutions? Although having S.A.F.E. goals should lead to success, lack of action can derail even the loftiest objectives.

In Lisa's first Women Moving Forward meeting, she heard of the "hits and misses" the women experienced with their goals. When the woman stated that she called three previous clients instead of six, she "missed" because she did not take action to contact the number of clients she said she would.

Think for a moment of a time when you said you would do something but didn't. What was the reason you didn't accomplish what you said you would? Could you have accomplished it had you consciously and purposefully committed to doing it? In most cases the answer is yes.

When we set goals that are S.A.F.E. nothing prevents success but lack of action. We see it in our own lives. We see it in our children's and other people's lives. Some may call it procrastination or lack of discipline. We simply call it lack of action.

When you set your goals, take conscious and deliberate action. Realize and accept that you need to do whatever it takes. Taking action allows you to move forward to your desired result.

"GETTING OFF THE POT"

One of the things I always wanted to do was belly dance. I knew it was something I could do; I just never followed through on my desire to learn it. Women Moving Forward was definitely the catalyst and it got me "off the pot." It helped me to see that it was something that I should no longer wait to do. It has helped me to keep the promise I made to myself, to be personally accountable for doing what I say to myself I will do.

Melanie is an entrepreneur who also came to the meetings at a transitional time in her life. She was recovering from depression and had just recently begun a business that was fuelled by her passion to bake.

Through one of the goal setting sessions at the Women Moving Forward meetings, Melanie's inner voice began to scream at her to get "off the pot," as she says it, to try belly dancing. Melanie's inner voice had been speaking to her for some time and she only now had started paying attention to it.

In listening to her spirit, Melanie affirmed her long held desire to learn to belly dance. She took action on her goal and has enjoyed its benefits. She recently completed her first four weeks of belly dancing and performed at a recital. Melanie admits that had she not taken action, she probably would not have experienced this long-time goal.

Taking action is the key to accomplishing your goals. And action requires a person to take initiative and step out of the comfort zone.

STEPPING OUT OF THE COMFORT ZONE

Everyone has doubts and fears. Only when we step out of our comfort zones or risk-free areas do we find ourselves truly moving forward in our lives.

Principle # 3: It won't get done unless you do it!

Joan is an entrepreneur who came to the meetings hoping to increase her business contacts. She discovered that she could step out of her comfort zone and achieve new and exciting goals that she had never even dreamed of.

Two of the speakers were truly inspirational to me. The president of a women's golfing association spoke about the importance of taking care of ourselves and how golfing could be a tool. She helped me realize that what she was offering could be for me. I had never golfed and it was never something I wanted to do. And yet, after hearing her speak, I was motivated to give golfing a shot! I have since enrolled in the program, a decision that would not have occurred had I not been willing to step out of my comfort zone. I'm looking forward to the new experience.

The second speaker also had an impact on me. A professional coach talked about the "Gremlins" that we deal with every day. We each have a Gremlin that tells us what to do and what not to do, and the trick is to tame the Gremlin. I quieted the Gremlin that told me I couldn't golf. After taming that Gremlin, I can see that joining a golfing association will benefit me both personally and professionally.

In reading Joan's story, we can clearly see the powerful impact stepping out of the comfort zone can have. Joan initially thought that golfing was something she couldn't do. Only when she made a decision to step out of her area of comfort did she find true satisfaction and joy in trying the new experience.

Joan also mentioned the negative voices that plagued her, the negative voices most people hear in their head. As the speaker put it, they are the "Gremlins" that people deal with every day. They pop up and put mental roadblocks in the path of action. These negative voices are powerful unless we can identify and tame them as Joan did. Once you hear them and notice that they are coming from your head and not your heart, you can silence them and move forward.

Joan was able to listen to her heart and move forward by stepping out of her comfort zone and joining the golfing association. She has taken action and is moving forward on her goal. She is living who she is. She is doing what she wants to do. And she is going where she wants to go. Her actions have allowed her to accomplish her goal and be successful. We congratulate Joan on her achievement.

What about you? What actions are you going to take? How will you "get off the pot" and "step out of your comfort zone" so you can move on to success?

Principle # 3: It won't get done unless you do it!

- *Get "off the pot" and just do it! Decide you will take action and do what you say you are going to do.*

- *Step out of your comfort zone and reap the rewards of taking action.*

- *Identify the mental roadblocks as they surface. Note that they are in your head, not in your heart, and move on.*

Principle # 4
Why do it alone?

BEING ABLE TO CREATE EXTRAORDINARY CHANGE is not an easy task. It requires listening to your heart to clearly identify who you are, and then aligning that with what you are doing to live your life with true passion and purpose. In creating your life roadmap and setting S.A.F.E. goals you can begin to create extraordinary change. You then follow this with action. You set and complete tasks that will bring you closer to achieving success.

There is one other element that Women Moving Forward offers. Support. Women Moving Forward recognizes that each woman is strong and unique and possesses her own internal support systems. Women Moving Forward also provides external support by encouraging and celebrating each of its members.

INTERNAL AND EXTERNAL SUPPORT SYSTEM

We all possess support systems to get us through times when we need a helping hand. Many are obvious, yet others are not.

Support systems are both internal and external. When identifying an internal support system, we must understand that it is not always obvious and may require mining the self to find it. Internal support systems are truly at the core of every human being. They are qualities people already possess that give them strength and power during difficult times. Those qualities are empowering as they fuel the tenacity to move forward.

An internal support system consists of qualities such as courage, grit, tenacity, resolve, persistence, doggedness, determination, belief in self and faith in outcomes.

Defining your own internal support system requires that you do an assessment of your strengths. You must look within and determine from past experiences what the qualities were that surfaced and got you through challenging times. Writing these down will give them more meaning and create your quality inventory.

When women share their accomplishments, I start to recognize in myself that I too may have achieved that same goal but never gave myself credit for achieving it. When you hear someone else accomplishing a goal that may be similar to a goal you set and accomplished before, you start to recognize more in yourself. It begins to confirm your own strengths.

Judi

Once your internal support system is identified, you will find yourself drawing from it more easily. You will begin to remind yourself of it during challenging times and you will get through these times more easily. This will help you move forward.

Because of what I was experiencing at the meetings, I believed in myself more than ever. I discovered a newfound belief in myself that I now tap into every day. I continue to pay attention to my inner strengths and push myself to do more.

Joan

Unlike internal support systems, external support systems involve other people. They are the people in your life who encourage and embrace you, and are there when the going

Principle # 4: Why do it alone?

gets tough. Identifying external support systems may seem easier to do than identifying internal ones, but this can be more difficult than it seems. There are external systems that can hinder the process, discourage your inner spirit and cause you to derail or abandon your goals.

Support systems need to be in line with who you are. They need to be available to support and encourage. If a support person does not believe in what you are doing, the support system is ineffective. It can be detrimental.

For a support system to work, it has to do just that, support. As with a bridge, the supports must be in place or the bridge will collapse. If a person's support system is not supporting them, their chances of success are greatly diminished.

IDENTIFYING THE RIGHT EXTERNAL SUPPORT SYSTEM

Identifying strong support systems requires you to ally yourself with like-minded people, people with similar strengths, abilities and beliefs. When you surround yourself with others who are similar, the support is stronger and often times most genuine. There is no competition or ill feeling. There is only support and encouragement.

I believe women need the support of other women. Being able to share my goals with other women and then have them recognize my accomplishments is very rewarding. The group's comments are always positive and there is a warm appreciation for each other's success.

Women struggle daily with eating properly, getting enough sleep and exercise. Then we must include maintaining healthy relationships with our spouse, children and work colleagues. When I attend a meeting and listen to other women's difficulties, I know I can make a difference by simply saying, "It's OK, I have been there and it too will pass," or "You may consider trying this route to simplify your life."

Some women need only to hear that they are not alone and that others have experienced the same situation. This reassures them and provides confidence to continue with a new approach or positive attitude to tackle the problems. Just knowing someone else was in a similar situation and survived is enough to permit that person to persevere. We help coach and encourage each other, and it is an opportune time to observe and hear the success and learn from the mistakes of others. Hearing other women's stories of their career journey reinforces my own belief that I also can achieve this level of success.

I am reenergized to hear I am not the only one who enjoys my job and all its many challenges. Initially I doubted myself and was planning for retirement, but now I am motivated to work for another 10 years just thinking of all the community activities, places to visit and people to meet – too much to do and no time to stagnate. All the positive energy is contagious.

Yvette is a woman who understands the importance of external support systems. Within the Women Moving Forward group, Yvette has come to appreciate the power women have when they support and connect with one another. There is mentoring, there is coaching, there is constant encouragement and support. Having this support system has allowed Yvette to move forward and believe that she too can achieve the level of success she desires.

Yvette also uses this support system to learn from others' experiences in order to avoid similar challenges. It has permitted Yvette to use the strengths of the group to fuel her own passions and desires. Because of the support she felt she discovered the desire to continue to work, a choice she made from within herself.

Principle # 4: Why do it alone?

Because of the belief I have in this support system, in the Women Moving Forward group, I have chosen to forward a copy of the weekly newsletter to other women, women who are unemployed or who are home on sick leave. They have expressed numerous times how grateful they are to feel part of the group, even when many have never been to a meeting.

This made me realize how valuable support with others is, especially when one is isolated. It makes people appreciate life from a different perspective by being grateful for all they possess and not what they are lacking!

My friends appreciated the stories in the newsletter and they are encouraged by all the kind and positive thoughts. This has motivated me to share my feelings and encourage others to do the same.

Yvette noticed the power of having a support system when she forwarded the newsletter to other women and to her surprise, several women wrote to her expressing their feelings of gratitude for allowing them to feel like they were part of the Women Moving Forward group, even when they had not been to a meeting.

This feeling of belonging, of being supported, has helped the other women because they could experience the power of the group and found appreciation for where they are in their lives.

Yvette has also come to appreciate the power of having a strong support system can be in achieving one's goals. The encouragement, recognition and celebration bring more strength to her spirit as she moves forward in her life.

As with Yvette, Judi has also experienced the benefits of having a strong support system. Judi came to Women Moving Forward looking to network with other businesswomen in the community.

The women of Women Moving Forward are what drive me to come back to the meetings. I love watching the women respond to the speakers and hear how Women Moving Forward has inspired them. Women are encouraged to share their experiences and I have noted that not one person dominates the conversation. Every one is provided an opportunity to share. And there is always a lot to cheer about and many successes to celebrate.

I am happy I have been part of such an incredible group of women, women who support each other, listen to each other and help one another. I seriously cannot see myself not being a part of this fantastic group. It is a part of my life, like going to church on Sundays. Women Moving Forward has become an important part of my life.

If you don't have personal access to Oprah or Dr. Phil, you should definitely join Women Moving Forward.

Judi loved the support she found in Women Moving Forward. She could identify with it and loved watching women grow and take action on their goals. The support women received at the meetings inspired Judi and drove her to keep coming. For Judi Women Moving Forward has become a part of her life, just like going to church on Sundays.

Many of us have other support systems— families, friends, colleagues, God, organizations we belong to, mentors and coaches. In being able to identify your own support systems, you can experience the successes of moving forward while feeling the support and encouragement of those who surround you.

Principle # 4: Why do it alone?

- *We all possess internal and external support systems.*

- *You have, within you right now, an internal support system willing and ready to help you move forward in your life.*

- *By recalling different experiences in your life, the glorious and successful to the challenging and difficult times, you can create an inventory of qualities that are already part of you and are your internal support system.*

- *An external support system is composed of the people and organizations that are in your life.*

- *Identify the like-minded and supportive people in your life right now.*

- *Seek the people who are genuinely interested in supporting and encouraging you to move forward.*

- *our external support system should encourage, inspire and motivate you.*

Principle # 5
The Promise of Change

IN ORDER TO CREATE the empowering and purposeful change that the women of Women Moving Forward have created, there is one more principle that will make your process complete. To recap, the first principle stressed the value of connecting with your self. The second involved creating powerful and meaningful S.A.F.E. goals. The third principle stressed the importance of taking action, and the fourth underlined the value of having strong internal and external support systems.

The fifth and last principle emphasizes the importance of creating a system that ensures your progress is on track. This is the ticket to realizing your goals and achieving extraordinary change and success.

In this chapter we will learn about the Promise of Change. This promise comes from within. It is a personal contract you set with yourself that encompasses the four other principles. This principle brings everything together.

TRACKING PROGRESS

The women of Women Moving Forward understand the importance of tracking their progress. They use the Goal Cards to write down their goals and they measure their accomplishments from one week to the next. Keeping an inventory of what they are doing and how it relates to who they are and where they are going allows them to move forward toward living their life with more passion and purpose.

Tracking is a mechanism to measure progress; it is a tool to evaluate, assess and review what you have done to ensure it is aligned with where you are going.

One of the ways to track is to follow up with yourself on a daily, weekly and monthly basis. At the Women Moving Forward meetings, the women set goals that can be achieved within a two-week period. Then they track these goals between meetings. At the following meeting, they share their accomplishments.

Because the goals are written, tracking is easy to do. It simply involves comparing action steps the women took with what they have or have not accomplished. Once the gaps are clear, they can then take steps to realign their goals and actions so that they move forward appropriately.

Tracking is effective because it allows you to realign your actions and goals early, before they can get derailed. It is far easier to realign yourself when you are still near your course. A slight shift can bring you back into alignment.

I have been using my goal cards to set my health and fitness goals since my first Women Moving Forward meeting. When my father passed away in April, I was very upset and found myself wanting to channel my grief. Rather than do something self-destructive, I decided to channel my grief into losing the extra weight I have been carrying for so long.

Having set Health and Fitness goals at each meeting has kept them top of mind. By having the weight loss as part of my goals week after week, when my father passed away, I knew this would be the perfect focus. In tracking my goals, I have since lost 25 pounds.— JUDI

If you do not track your progress, you cannot clearly and systematically measure your success. It's like travelling on a

Principle # 5: The promise of change

roadway that has no signs showing the distance left to travel. You cannot be certain how close or how far you are to reaching your destination.

As with the other principles we've seen thus far, the workbook at the end of the book can help you move forward to create empowering and purposeful change. The workbook has a 90-Day Action Plan to help you to track your goals daily, weekly and monthly. You can then evaluate your progress, and see how well you are progressing toward success.

BEING RESPONSIBLE FOR YOUR "SELF"

The second part of the Promise of Change involves being truly honest with yourself and being accountable. Although accountability may seem like a strong word, the women of Women Moving Forward have come to embrace it. They have come to enjoy the benefits of being responsible and answerable to themselves and others. They realize the absolute necessity of being accountable to themselves. They understand accountability's role in ensuring successful outcomes. They hold themselves responsible for their own actions.

We have also noticed the importance of being accountable to your external support system. The women enjoy sharing their goals with the other women. It increases the odds of their success and adds importance to the outcome. They understand and embrace the importance of sharing their goals with the others and they know that the women will give them unbiased support and encouragement. By sharing their goals, they create an even larger support system, one that lifts and carries them through the process.

Being accountable to others is a powerful thing.

What keeps me coming back is the personal accountability I get from the meetings. From writing down my goals, to sharing them with the others, I get a strong sense of accomplishment and that is due to the personal accountability I feel.

It is always fun to look back on your previous goals and fess up to the goals you said you would do and haven't done, and it's great to celebrate and be recognized for what you did accomplish. Being accountable has been wonderful – it has helped me achieve many different things. — MELANIE

By sharing with other women, by seeing and feeling each other's success, being accountable has a powerful impact and shows other women that you truly can reach your goals and be successful. It helps women to see that they can do something more. That it is possible. And the results are real. The domino effect is that the women before them will inspire other women. — RACHEL

I have been motivated and inspired by the women. Hearing other women share their experience has made me want to share mine and become more involved. I want to make new friends, I want to make new business contacts, and I want to grow personally. By sharing with others, I have been inspired to do what I wanted to do. I am more confident and able to achieve the goals I set for myself. — SUSAN

Each woman has experienced the power of accountability. Sharing with the other women has allowed them to stay true to their own goals while being inspired to desire more for themselves.

By being accountable, you are responsible for actions not taken and can re-evaluate your goal and your progress. Necessary steps to get back on track can naturally follow.

Being accountable is a wonderful tool in achieving extraordinary success. It starts by being accountable to your self, doing what you say you will do, and then tracking your progress by reviewing your goals regularly.

Having a strong support system in which you are accountable is very helpful in moving forward. Being accountable to others permits support and encouragement and also brings recognition and celebration to your life.

Principle # 5: The Promise of Change

- *Stay true to yourself by making the commitment to continually move forward in your life.*

- *Track your progress daily, weekly and monthly. Review your goals consistently and regularly.*

- *If you find yourself moving away from a goal, re-evaluate it and ensure it is aligned with your inner self.*

- *Be accountable to yourself and to others. Share your goals and involve your external support system in your journey to move forward.*

What are you waiting for?

AS I SIT HERE WRITING this chapter of the book, my heart aches with the reality of the news I just recently received. It's the news you dread hearing, the news that changes everything. Although it is not directly related to Women Moving Forward, it certainly is in line with helping you create extraordinary and empowering change.

My sister-in-law went in for surgery to remove a cyst she had felt growing inside of her. During the surgery, all our lives changed. They found cancer. The doctor performed emergency surgery, carefully removing the large cyst and several malignant tumours. The news was not delivered to her until the following morning.

I can't imagine how the doctor felt as he faced her to relate the news. I can't imagine the faces of my sister-in-law and her husband of 21 years as they heard the words the doctor told them. All I can envision are sombre faces, ones filled with shock, disbelief and pure horror that my sister-in-law may be losing her life. Losing her life; the life she had been living freely without the feeling of darkness of death. My eyes swell with tears as I look at her face, one that is filled with the fear of the unknown; the fear that she may only have a little time left before she becomes but a memory to the rest of us.

And as I feel her pain in my own heart, I become filled with the same fear. The fear is so powerful that it overtakes me as I envision my family without me. I look at my nine-year-old son and see how powerful a man he will be; so thoughtful and caring and so willing to help others. I look at my six-year-old daughter and see a beautiful woman who will nourish the people in her life. And I look at my husband and see a man whose love for me is beyond words.

I look at my family as they go about their activities and I remove myself from the picture. Oh, does that hurt! It hurts to think that I too could be taken from them and I would not get to experience all that could be.

As my sister-in-law faces this new reality in her life, it brings new perspective to all of us. The burning question in my mind is "Why wait? Why wait to hear such devastating news to realize that life is precious and it should be handled with care?" And that care can only come from inside, from wanting to live a fulfilling life, one that is enriched by all that we can enjoy.

When we placed our hand on our heart, we reconnected with our 'self'. We became grounded and could listen to our inner voice. If we took the time to pay careful attention, we were able to hear our innermost self.

Up until this point, we have journeyed through the lives of other women. We have shared in their triumphs of self-discovery and success. Now it's time to get serious, to really understand our true passion and purpose and start to take the steps to move forward.

This next step may dramatically change your perception of where you are today and push you to evaluate your life and make the important decision to move forward. The next process may also help you create more calmness in your life, calmness that is grounded in your focus on what is important to you.

THE VALUE OF TIME

Time is a luxury. We often hear people say "There is not enough time during the day," or "I wish I had more time." But the reality is, there is plenty of time, and there are many wonderful moments waiting to happen. People get so caught up in the busy-ness of being busy that they fail to see the value of the time they actually do have.

If you were given the same news today that my sister-in-law received, how would that affect the way you value time? Think about it. Envision yourself in a room with just you and the doctor. The room is tense with the darkness of the news that is to be delivered to you. The doctor has *that* look on his face, the one that says that what he will say will forever change your life.

You look into his eyes and know there is something wrong. You can sense it in the core of your being. You hope for the best but you know that what will be said will be hard to hear.

As he begins to speak, you feel an ever-increasing sense of desperation and urgency. Your heart is racing and you don't want to be in this room. It can't be happening to you. You wish it were all a dream.

And when you finally hear the doctor say it, your life flashes before you. Your heart sinks. You feel ill. You want to vomit. You want to run. You want it all to be a mistake. But it's not. And you are now facing the fact that your life will forever be changed.

Close the book for a moment and put your hand on your heart. Think of what you just read and feel the words that the doctor has just said. Think of your family. Think of what they are doing right now and what is to come in their lives. Think of all the things you would miss if your life were cut short. Now feel it in your heart. Feel all the pain that comes with knowing you can be removed from the life you are now living. Feel it in the deepest part of your soul.

Now feel what is happening to you. Feel the resistance of facing this image. Feel it and let it come to the surface. Let it push itself through as it becomes more and more powerful. This is what is known as the will to survive, the "why" in our lives.

When a person has a powerful reason to live, a powerful "why," the world opens up to them and they move forward with greater ease. It is important to grab hold of your "why" and let it be the hand in the small of your back, gently guiding you to move forward in your life.

Why do people have to hear such terrible news before they begin to realize the power of the time they have? From the moment we are born, we are dying. Why do people not live that way? Why do so many waste precious time? Why do so many live lives unaware of who they truly are? Isn't it only when people are living their true self that they are living their best life?

Where are you today? Are you living the life you dreamed you could be living? Are you living the life you want to live? What choices have you made that prevent you from living a life that is true to who you are?

The women we have met have experienced something unique. They have realized and taken advantage of the opportunity to live their lives true to who they are because they chose to realize it. These women started making choices by listening to their true selves. This brought calmness to their lives as they focused on what was important to them.

You have time. You have plenty of time. You have today. And by focusing on what is important to you, by having the "why" in your life that gently urges you forward, you can begin to value the time you have. And that value of time is the gift you have. It's a gift we all have. We simply have to acknowledge it and make it count.

Remember yourself in that doctor's office. How much would the things you are doing in your life change? Would you be happy with what you are doing and have accomplished? Would you be proud of the way you have lived your life and what you have given to others? Or do you have regrets? Do you feel you could have done more? Do you feel you wasted too much of your time doing the things that didn't matter to you?

Now realize that today is yours for the taking. Ground yourself by placing your hand on your heart and listen to what your inner self is saying. Listen to what it is saying as if you were in a place that was overshadowed by your own mortality. It is powerful to take a hold of time and become a master of it. Time does not control you – you control it. Grasp it. Use the time you have by making conscious choices every day to live the life you want to live.

If you truly listen to your heart, your inner being, the "doing" will come naturally. The "doing" will be in line with your own life's purpose. If you haven't determined what that is yet, place yourself back in the doctor's office and listen to the bad news. What will you do with the rest of your life? What is important to you?

Many who are faced with their own mortality become clearer about their life's purpose. Time for them is precious and there is no wasting a minute of it. Their life has new meaning and it drives them to continue moving forward.

What are the things you can do today to take action on living your life more aligned with your own inner spirit, with who you are? You need to know where you are going and it's time to create the roadmap that encompasses all that your inner spirit is, all that you are.

Follow me into the next chapter as we move forward and create your first 90-day roadmap to empowering and extraordinary success!

The 90-day Empowerment Action Plan workbook

AT THE BEGINNING OF THE BOOK, you were told you were holding the key that would open doors to extraordinary change for you. You were told that you were going to be guided through the process that other women, like yourself, have experienced to create extraordinary and purposeful change in their lives. You were told you were going to meet ordinary women who found their inner selves and are now living their lives with more passion and purpose.

You do have the key to open the door to extraordinary change. You always had it. The purpose of the book was meant to be a mirror for you and your own life. It was meant to allow you to gaze at the life you are currently living and decide for yourself how you can begin to start living your life with more passion and purpose.

This book is also intended to inspire you through the stories of the women of Women Moving Forward. Their stories are meant to encourage you, to motivate you and to allow you to feel like you too can do it. You too can create extraordinary and purposeful change. Like the women in the stories, you too can live your life with more passion and purpose.

While reading the book, you were able to look at your life, listen to your inner self and see if the life you are living is aligned with who you truly are.

The book was not meant to cause a complete life overhaul but to gently place a guiding hand on your back to move you forward in a direction that better nourishes who you truly are. The reality is that you have the power to make things happen. You can envision what you would like your life to be like. You know what your "self" is saying, what motivates, inspires, excites and empowers you. And you can do something about it.

The next part of the book will be the "working" part. It is meant to get you thinking, writing and moving forward by taking action, almost as though you were taking part in a Women Moving Forward meeting.

ACTION WORKSHEETS—The "How to" for the "To do"

The Action Worksheets are a gift for you to begin taking action. Use them to plan, map out, and create your first 90-day empowerment action plan. Take all the time you need to fill in the worksheets and get excited with the process.

What you are about to create is a roadmap to living your life with more passion and purpose. It's your path to extraordinary and empowering change in your life.

THE FIRST STEP: Who "Am I?" worksheets

The women of Women Moving Forward have come to discover their inner selves, to listen and pay attention. By doing the "Who Am I?" exercise, you are tuning into who you are, your inner self, in order to create your plan to live your life with more passion and empowerment. If you haven't already done the exercise in Chapter Four – Reconnecting With The Self, here is your opportunity to do it.

Use this worksheet to fill in the answers that surface as you listen to your inner voice. Sit quietly and relax. Listen attentively using all of your senses, without judging or dismissing what surfaces. Take your time and fill in the pages, colouring them with as much detail as possible

Once you have completed the worksheets, highlight or circle words or themes that recur. Your strongest and most enjoyable skills, abilities, strengths and activities will emerge. As you notice that these paint a picture, you will feel yourself becoming excited. This is when you start to truly see what nourishes you.

As you continue to evaluate and put reoccurring themes together, you will envision a life that encompasses all that you are, all that you enjoy, all that empowers you. You awaken your passion and define your purpose.

Some of you are already living your purpose. Others may find yourselves wanting to take action to add more of the things that bring joy into your life.

Here is one note of caution. Do not feel as if you have to change your entire life. Remember, you are exactly where you are supposed to be. It's been a natural process for you in your life to get to where you are today. Accept and embrace it. The point is to start realizing that there many things you can be doing that would be more aligned with who you truly are.

STEP TWO: *My life's passion and purpose*

The next worksheet, "My Life's Passion & Purpose" will help you clearly define some of the things you can begin doing today to take action and move forward.

The worksheet helps you write affirming statements that will guide you to creating your 90-day action plan.

The first question, "Today I am" requires that you define the person you are by using the personality traits you circled or highlighted in the previous worksheet. In one or two sentences, list the person that you are. The objective is to encourage and move you forward by focusing on the positive.

"I am passionate about" is a question to solidify what empowers your spirit. What are the things you do that light your fire. Again, refer to the previous worksheet.

"I am already living my passion and purpose" is to ensure you acknowledge and celebrate what you are already doing that is aligned with your passion and purpose. List the things that you are already doing and living that nourish you and empower you.

"My ultimate goal is to be able to . . . because…" is a statement that brings into focus your long-term vision of how you see yourself living your life with passion and purpose every single day. It's almost like saying, "If money were no object, this is what I would be doing because it would nourish me, fuel me, inspire and motivate me, and completely fulfill me".

THIRD STEP: *My support systems*

As we saw earlier, having strong support systems enable us to move forward successfully. They help us get through challenges and obstacles and allow us to be accountable and celebrate along the way. Without our support systems, moving forward is difficult. Everyone already has support systems in place. It's a matter of acknowledging who they are and how they can help us.

The "Support Systems" worksheet helps you identify and acknowledge the internal and external support systems in your life. Your Internal Support System, as described in Chapter Seven, is the list of personality traits you possess that help you get through challenging and difficult times. Your list consists of qualities such as courage, grit, tenacity, resolve, persistence, doggedness, determination, belief in self, and faith in outcomes.

As you list your qualities, think back to times when you needed to work through a challenge or a difficult moment in your life. What are some of the personality traits you possess that got you through? Write everything down as you take inventory of your internal support system.

Once you are finished, review the list and enjoy what you see. You have a powerful internal support system already in you that is available for you to tap into when you need it. Refer to this list often and add new traits as you become aware of them.

The external support system consists of the people in your life that you can turn to for help and guidance. Examples of external support people are family, friends, colleagues, God, organizations you belong to, mentors, coaches and the women of Women Moving Forward.

There are countless people in our lives but list only those whom you feel you can truly turn to for support. List only those with whom you'd feel comfortable sharing your vision for yourself. These are the right kind of people you want to list as being part of your external support system. Of course you can add names of new support people as they enter your life.

MY PERSONAL ROADMAP—The action plan

At every meeting, the women of Women Moving Forward set goals that focus on what's important in their lives. Without the goals, the action to move forward would be vague. By setting clear actionable goals, the women begin to realize the power of each goal as it is accomplished. By taking action, the women move forward toward living the life they desire.

MY 90-DAY ACTION PLAN WORKSHEET

This worksheet is your canvas. You will use it to paint the picture of what you would like to accomplish in the next ninety days.

The three categories listed are the ones the women of Women Moving Forward have been using to create extraordinary and empowering change.

The first category is *Health & Fitness*. We all agree that if you are not healthy you have difficulty getting through some of life's daily activities. We therefore focus on health and fitness as our priority. We emphasize creating small changes, one week at a time, to improve our health and our fitness.

For us, health means the internal functioning of our system and what we put in it to fuel it. We set goals for healthier eating, more rest and less stress, we focus on doing things that nourish who we are.

Our fitness goal is the action, the movement we do to keep us healthy. It's not about exercising to look good, it's about exercising to feel good. The benefits of physical activity have been proven in countless studies and we all know we should be doing some. However, we let other priorities and other people's priorities get in the way of our own physical fitness. Therefore, we consciously take initiative to add physical activity to our daily lives to feel better.

The next category of goals centres on where we spend most of our waking time during the day – working. Whether we are employed by someone else, work for ourselves or are homemakers, we work, and we spend most of our time in this area of our lives. Having a strong and clear focus on what we want to be doing with this time is important. It relates to living our life with passion and purpose. By being able to spend our waking hours doing what we are passionate about, at least in one form or another, we are able to feel empowered and excited about our life.

As you can see, setting strong *Business & Career* goals is important. These goals keep your daily activities in focus. They help you determine whether your daily activities are truly moving you forward in the direction you want to be heading.

When setting *Business & Career* goals, as with any goals, understand and acknowledge the reason for setting these goals. Being clear on the "why" behind each goal gives it power. Remember that S.A.F.E. goals lead to success. Make sure your goals come from within, from your self, that they are aligned with what you want to accomplish, and are focused on clear objectives that empower and excite you.

The third category is *Humanitarian* goals. Often when we think of someone being humanitarian, we think of them donating their time to volunteer or donating money to a charity. We see them giving of themselves to someone else.

Being humanitarian, however, means much more than that. It really means being caring, compassionate, kind and loving to other human beings. It does not come with a price tag nor does it require giving of one's self to someone else.

When the women of Women Moving Forward set their humanitarian goals, it really brings into focus how they add caring and compassionate acts to their daily lives without adding more stress or costing more money. Humanitarian goals can be as simple as doing one unselfish act for someone else, doing a good deed without recognition, or sending a "thinking of you" card to a friend who's going through a difficult time. Being humanitarian simply means being aware that you can be more caring and compassionate.

THE MONTHLY PICTURE

In order to paint a clear 90-day picture of what you are going to accomplish, you need to know what the three 30-day periods will look like. What do you want to have accomplished after each four week period? Break down your goals into thirds and write them down in the appropriate columns.

You will then use these columns to plan your weekly strategy. What will you do each week that will get you to your 30-day goal, which will eventually lead you to accomplishing your 90-day goal? On a monthly basis, break down your goal into quarters and visualize your weekly outcome for each goal. Write them down on the next worksheet called "Weekly Action Plan – Week #".

The bottom of the worksheet requires you to make a commitment to yourself. Commit to taking action on the goals you have set and add significance to your own accountability. Be true to yourself and commit with your entire heart and being.

WEEKLY ACTION PLAN

The weekly action plan gives you a clear picture of the goals you need to accomplish to realize your monthly goal. It's the best tool to plan your workweek.

On your Weekly Action Plan, for the first week write Week #1. Refer to the quarterly goals you set for your first month and write in the goals you will accomplish your first week. Ensure they are goals that are S.A.F.E. and will lead you directly to the outcome you are working toward.

You will then use this Weekly Action Plan to create your Daily Action Plan. Every week you have a set number of goals. What are the tasks you need to accomplish to achieve your goals? Break your plan down into five or six days you will use to accomplish your goals.

You will note that the Weekly and Daily Action Plans keep you focused on the big picture, the 'why' for each of your goals and their tasks. Knowing what you are working towards keeps it fresh, keeps it alive, keeps you moving in the direction you are wanting to go. It is so much easier to stay aligned with your goals when you know exactly where you are going. It's clear and it's focused.

On each of the Weekly and Daily Action Plans you will also find a place to include affirmations as to what you are proud of. This is an important part of the process. It's the recognition you can give yourself every day to motivate and inspire you to continue. It's your daily pat on the back, recognition you deserve and rarely receive.

The interesting thing that happens when you use the 90-Day Action Plan is that it becomes your personal journal. It diarizes your activities and your accomplishments and gives you something to look back on and be proud of. There is space to make notes and write comments to your self. It becomes your journal of success.

But here are a few words of caution. Do not expect any results unless you are truly committed and intend to follow through. You can make it happen. You can live your life with more passion and purpose. And you can create extraordinary and empowering change. You can! But you must commit to taking action. You must commit to the truth of the outcome. If you fail to take action, you accept to fail to accomplish. Only you can move yourself forward.

Most women have been on a diet or have followed an exercise plan and failed. Why? Because they were not committed to the outcome. They failed to realize that by not taking action they were accepting to not succeed. It may sound harsh but that is the reality.

Commit to yourself that every day you will do the little things that will get you to the big things, the life of empowerment and fulfillment. Creating your 90-Day Empowering Action Plan will lead you to fulfil the goals of your dreams.

Like the women of Women Moving Forward, you are reconnecting with your self. You are setting S.A.F.E. goals and you are taking action. You are identifying and utilizing your own internal and external support systems and tracking your progress while staying committed and accountable to yourself. You are creating extraordinary and empowering change. You have the ability and the tools to succeed. Go for it!

The 90-day Empowerment Action Plan workbook

STEP ONE: Who am I?

My personality traits

_____

_____

_____

My qualities

_____

_____

_____

What I enjoy doing

_____

_____

_____

What fulfills me

_____

_____

_____

_____

What excites me

What I am passionate about

What I desire

My strengths

What empowers me

The 90-day Empowerment Action Plan workbook

When I feel my best, I am...

_____

_____

_____

What I am most happy, I am....

_____

_____

_____

I am different from everyone else because I...

_____

_____

_____

I want people to remember me for who I am, and that is....

_____

_____

_____

I want people to say that I am....

_____

_____

STEP TWO: My Life's Passion and Purpose — What am I doing? Where am I going?

Today I am

_____

_____

_____

I am passionate about

_____

_____

_____

I am already living my passion and purpose by

_____

_____

_____

My ultimate goal is to be able to

_____

_____

because then I know I'll be living my life with passion and purpose.

STEP THREE: My Support Systems

INTERNAL SUPPORT SYSTEM   **EXTERNAL SUPPORT SYSTEM**

_____   _____

_____   _____

_____   _____

_____   _____

_____   _____

_____   _____

_____   _____

_____   _____

STEP FOUR: 90-DAY GOALS

For the next 90 days, I am committed to:

_____

_____

_____

_____

STEP FOUR continued on page 78

STEP FOUR—Part 1 of 3: First 30 Days

HEALTH & FITNESS

Weight _____

Cholesterol Level _____

Fat % _____

Measurements _____

Other _____

BUSINESS & CAREER

Project #1 _____

Project #2 _____

Project #3 _____

Income _____

Commissions _____

Sales _____

Other _____

HUMANTIRIAN

Charitable Organization _____

Volunteer Hours _____

Funds to be donated _____

Good deeds _____

OTHER

_____

STEP FOUR continued on page 79

STEP FOUR—Part 2 of 3: First 60 Days

HEALTH & FITNESS

Weight _____

Cholesterol Level _____

Fat % _____

Measurements _____

Other _____

BUSINESS & CAREER

Project #1 _____

Project #2 _____

Project #3 _____

Income _____

Commissions _____

Sales _____

Other _____

HUMANTIRIAN

Charitable Organization _____

Volunteer Hours _____

Funds to be donated _____

Good deeds _____

OTHER

_____

STEP FOUR continued on page 80

STEP FOUR—Part 3 of 3: 90 Days

HEALTH & FITNESS

Weight _____

Cholesterol Level _____

Fat % _____

Measurements _____

Other _____

BUSINESS & CAREER

Project #1 _____

Project #2 _____

Project #3 _____

Income _____

Commissions _____

Sales _____

Other _____

HUMANTIRIAN

Charitable Organization _____

Volunteer Hours _____

Funds to be donated _____

Good deeds _____

OTHER

_____

The 90-day Empowerment Action Plan workbook

STEP FIVE—Part 1 of 2: Weekly Action Plan
Week # _____

THIS WEEK I WIL:	THIS MONTH'S GOAL	90 DAY GOAL
HEALTH & FITNESS		
BUSINESS & CAREER		
HUMANTIRIAN		
OTHER A		
OTHER B		

This week, I am proud that I ...

STEP FIVE—Part 2 of 2: Daily Action Plan

Day # _____

TODAY I WILL:	THIS MONTH'S GOAL	90 DAY GOAL
HEALTH & FITNESS		
BUSINESS & CAREER		
HUMANTIRIAN		
OTHER A		
OTHER B		

Today, I am proud that I ...

Epilogue
How to become one of us

THE WEEKLY WOMEN MOVING FORWARD newsletter offers tips and helpful information in the three aspects of focus: *Health and Fitness, Business and Career* and *Humanitarianism*. The information in the newsletter will help keep you educated and inspired. New members are featured and their stories are shared. Like in the book, success stories are part of the newsletter to help motivate and inspire you.

You can become part of the online community being developed at www.WomenMovingForward.ca. It's a virtual meeting place that is geared to help and support you along the way. As the community grows, so will the success stories.

And best of all, you can become a Women Moving Forward member and participate weekly at meetings, meetings that focus on creating an empowering and nourishing atmosphere for you. The meetings are now becoming "me" time for so many of the members. It has become their time to take care of themselves, to nourish themselves and to get away from it all. The meeting is where it all truly comes together; women sharing their goals and their accomplishments, women inspiring and encouraging one another and speakers educating and motivating. And you can become part of it.

For information on how to participate in or become a member of a Women Moving Forward group in your area, see our website at www.WomenMovingForward.ca, or contact us at: info@WomenMovingForward.ca.

About the Author
Pierrette Raymond

Pierrette has been married to Luc for 11 years and has two children, Joshua, 9, and Briana, 6. Both she and her husband were born and raised in Timmins, Ontario and moved to Ottawa in 2000. She and her family have appreciated and enjoyed the many opportunities the nation's capital has had to offer since their move.

Pierrette has been actively helping women for the past 13 years as a teacher, recruiter, trainer, and mentor. She continues to live her life's passion to teach and make a difference in the lives of others by inspiring and motivating them to live life with true passion.

She founded Women Moving Forward in October 2002 to further find balance in her own life, while offering the same opportunity to other women. It has been the most rewarding time of her life as she has helped many women find their own inner voice, one that inspires to live life to their fullest ability. Her mission is to continue to offer women an opportunity to grow through education, experience and inspiration.

Pierrette has a strong desire to continually nourish her mind and is an avid reader. Her most precious time is spent with her children who she feels are growing up much too fast. Together, they spend their time biking, playing sports, and cuddling on the couch every Sunday for family day. Her vision for Women Moving Forward is to have women across North America living their life's true potential because they too have found what they needed to nourish them in their lives.

Participant Biographies

HERE IS SOME BIOGRAPHICAL INFORMATION on the women who so generously agreed to share their stories.

Yvette Petersen, B.Sc.N., MBA
Regional Coordinator Canada Post Project, Medisys

Yvette Petersen has been married for over 25 years and has three adult daughters aged 27, 24 and 21. She is originally from the Windsor area and moved to Thunder Bay, Ontario after graduating from Windsor University with a Bachelor of Science in Nursing. She completed her MBA in 2000 at the University of Ottawa.

She is currently employed as the Regional Coordinator for Ottawa and Eastern Ontario with *MEDISIS* Health Care Group Inc.

She enjoys mountain biking, walking, gardening, traveling and reading. Over the years, she has become involved as a volunteer in many sports clubs to promote girls in sports. She joined Women Moving Forward in order to share her community, her career and her family experiences with other women. She is constantly seeking new techniques to problem solve and develop coping strategies. She enjoys learning and hearing how other women succeed.

Carmen Perron

Carmen is the mother of three children 16, 18 and 20 and has been married to Mike for 23 years. She is from a small town, North Bay, Ontario and is one of the youngest of a family of

10 other siblings. She considers her family her number one priority in her life.

Carmen has 12 years experience in IT Technical and Business Development and is presently working in the Adaptive Computer Technology at Environment Canada.

As a recent community involvement, she has accepted the challenge in joining Wired Women Society (WWS) as Director of Mentorship, coordinating a Peer2Peer Program.

Carmen is a strong believer in continuous self-directed learning and hopes to implement resources to acquire personal and specialized empowerment within herself and others.

She enjoys sports and has a very strong interest in nutrition. She also enjoys boating, which allows her to enjoy her love of nature. Carmen is a strong believer in doing what you are passionate about.

Tel.: 613-837-5739
Email: CPerron@rogers.com
Website: http://www.wiredwoman.com/ottawa/peer2peer

Joan Jesion

Independent Advanced Director for the Pampered Chef Canada, Ltd.

Joan began her career with The Pampered Chef in 1996 because she was looking for a career that would meet her needs for flexibility, income and enjoyment of working with people. She is excited about her career because not only does she work around her family's schedule but she helps others get started in their own fun and fulfilling careers. She also loves demonstrating quick and easy meal solutions to other busy families and well as teaching people that the art of entertaining need not be overwhelming. "People should enjoy the time spent around the table with family and friends. It is absolutely the best way to connect with people so the right tools just make prep time fun!" She looks forward to many more years of helping others reach their professional goals with the unlimited potential of owning one's own business while enjoying the many rewards of building a wonderful business network.

Joan has been married over 25 years and has two busy teenage boys, one with special needs and two small dogs. As well as cooking, she enjoys reading, scrap booking and travel.

Tel.: (613) 830-1716
Email: joanjesion@rogers.com
Website: www.pamperedchef.com

Judith Cane, RHU
Wealth Strategies, Financial Planner

Judith lives in Orleans, Ontario with her husband Ian Fisher and 7 year-old son Sam, Schooner the golden retriever, Ruby the cat and an as yet unnamed kitten.

Judith has been teaching women how to balance their lives by giving them the financial tools to achieve their goals for over 10 years. She provides outstanding customer service by working primarily with women who have investment assets of $100,000 or more. She provides customized, comprehensive financial plans as well as detailed reviews, investment management, insurance strategies and succession planning for family estates and businesses.

She is an avid quilter and is past president of The Common Thread Quilt Guild in Orleans, founder of The Quilters' Workshop and the Ontario Representative for the Canadian

Quilters Association. Judith and her family have a cottage on Lac Ste. Marie used all year for skiing, golf and water sports.

Tel.: 613-841-8550
Email: judith@wsplanning.com
Web Address: www.wsplanning.com

Melanie Arscott
Owner of Mennie's Homemade Treats & Sweets

A child of the '60s, (with a little hippie still in her heart), Melanie was born in Montreal, Quebec. Married to her college sweetheart, Melanie and Martin now have two adolescent sons (along with a rabbit, a bird, two frogs and four fish). A long career in marketing ended in 2002 when she decided to stay home, spend more time with her children and make more cookies.

What began as a hobby in the late '80s has grown to a considerable business. And as for the future, well, we'll just have to wait and see... She enjoys genealogy and baking.

Tel.: (613) 733-3771 or 296-3091
Email: mennies@sympatico.ca

Pauline Fleming
PRO-Active Possibilities
Personal and Professional Coach/Speaker

Pauline is the founder and owner of PRO-Active Possibilities, a coaching company offering success and work/life balance solutions through coaching, speaking and retreats. Her clients achieve focus and positive results with her support as their accountability partner. She specializes in time and self-leadership—eliminating overwhelm by getting organized.

She partners with time-starved executives, entrepreneurs and coaches to take their lives and their businesses to the next level. Having it all is just the beginning!

Participants leave her customized retreats and speaking presentations wanting to know when the next one will be—re-energized and reconnected with what's really important!

Pauline holds a Masters degree in Leisure Service Administration—combining the best of leadership and wellness. She completed her coach training through Coach University, and as a member of the International Coaching Federation, she is working towards her Master Certified Coach designation—the highest designation in the world.

Pauline's motto is: Live, Love, Laugh and Learn; then lead others to do the same!

Tel.: 613-729-4765
Email: coach@paulinefleming.com
Web Address: www.paulinefleming.com

Susan Ebbs
Owner Total Renewal

Susan was born in Winnipeg, Manitoba, but moved to Ottawa, Ontario as a young girl, and has lived here ever since. Susan completed her Medical Secretarial Diploma at Algonquin College. She has two teenage daughters and a common-law partner, who have lived in Ottawa South for the past three years. Her love for animals is evident since she has two dogs, two cats, one guinea pig, one mouse and two love birds.

Susan Ebbs has 25 years experience in the medical field, working at many hospitals, doctors' offices, government departments and private industry. She is now owner of Total

Renewal, giving people an opportunity to shop on-line from the comfort of their own home for preventative healthcare products. Total Renewal is affiliated with NuSkin Canada, who are dedicated to providing the finest natural self-care products.

Susan also owns Sue's Prompt Processing for the past 17 years, and provides dictatyping from regular, mini or micro-cassettes of symposia, medical reports in both official languages, desktop publishing and database management. Her main client is CHEO (Children's Hospital of Eastern Ontario). Sue's Prompt Processing also has a facility security clearance to Secret II.

Since joining Women Moving Forward, Susan has tried out new experiences—participating in a best ball golf tournament (something she has never done). She has also made many meaningful business and personal friendships with other members. Women Moving Forward have as their mandate health, humanitarianism and exercise. This fits perfectly into what Susan has been able to accomplish in the past year—losing 33 pounds, increasing her exercising by walking more, and eating more fruits and vegetables, and generally improving her health. Susan has also signed up to sponsor needy children in Third World countries through the Nourish the Children Initiative. Over the past few weeks of the summer, she has been corresponding with a couple of ladies in the Summer Buddy Program. This is a fantastic way to get to know the members on a more personal level, and adds to the support to carry on with their goals.

Tel.: 260-9180 or 877-738-7059
Email: totalrenewal@rogers.com
Web Address: www.totalrenew.mypharmanex.com